GLENN VAN EKEREN

PLAY BOOK

T0164516

STRATEGIES
FOR BEING
A
STANDOUT
PERFORMER

HIGHERLIFE
DEVELOPMENT SERVICES, INC

Playbook: Strategies for Being a Standout Performer
by Glenn Van Ekeren

Published by HigherLife Publishing and Marketing
400 Fontana Circle
Building 1, Suite 105
Oviedo, Florida 32765
(407) 563-4806
www.ahigherlife.com

ISBN 13: 978-1-939183-25-5

Cover Design: Doni Keene

First Edition

14 15 16 17 18 — 9 8 7 6 5 4 3 2 1
Printed in the United States of America

DEDICATION

This book is dedicated to all the fabulous people I work with everyday who believe in and love what they do. They are truly Standout Performers and I celebrate their influence on my life and their success.

TABLE OF CONTENTS

CHAPTER 1

BECOME AN EXPERT AT WHAT YOU DO

I N HIS BOOK, *Principle-Centered Leadership*, Stephen M.R. Covey tells how Christopher Columbus was once invited to a banquet, where he was seated at the most honorable place at the table. A superficial self-seeker who was insanely jealous of Columbus asked him pointedly, "Had you not discovered the Indies, are there not other men in Spain who would have been capable of the enterprise?"

Rather than reply, Columbus took an egg and invited those around him to make it stand on end. They all attempted, but in vain; whereupon he tapped it on the table denting one end, and left it standing.

> There are two types of people in the business community; those who produce results and those who give you reasons why they didn't.
> —PETER DRUCKER

"We all could have done it that way!" the courtier accused.

"Yes, if you had only known how," replied Columbus. "And once I showed you the way to the New World, nothing was easier than to follow it."

It's much easier to follow the path to achievement than to blaze the path yourself. True explorers venture into unchartered territory knowing full well it would be much easier if they waited for someone else to show the way.

High achievers tend to be dreamers, and that's a good thing. But there is a distinct gap between a notion and accomplishment, revelation and achievement, inspiration and productivity. Lots of people have great ideas in the shower, but rare are those who dry off and do something about them. In order to reap the benefits of any brilliant idea, you must find a way to bridge the gaps. Bridging the gap between concept and practical application excites initiators.

As Zig Ziglar so eloquently said, "You don't have to be great to start, but you have to start to be great."

Disturb the Present. When was the last time you did something for the first time? Refuse to get comfortable with being comfortable. Be restless. Push on. Discover something other than the tried and true.

Drive Intentional Improvement. Initiators are rarely satisfied with the way things are. Give yourself permission to discover and experiment. Find a crack, a slight opening in the 'ordinary' and create the extraordinary. Move from blind satisfaction to a chronic, obsessive, compulsive passion for making things better.

Determine Your Path. Do you want to make a difference with your life? Do you want the world, your family, your work, relationships to be better because of you? Stop waiting for someone to create a risk-proof plan to make it happen. Create it!

Put your energies, ideas – your heart – into the world and people around you. Uncover undiscovered possibilities because, like Columbus, you were willing to go first into unchartered territory. Be an initiator.

BECOME AN EXPERT AT WHAT YOU DO

Experts. Who are they?

Experts do what they do like no one else can do it. Make that your mantra. Do what you do like no one else does it!

The morning after the big Heisman Trophy ceremony the newspaper headline read: "A landmark night for Baylor." Baylor's junior quarterback Robert Griffin III became the school's first Heisman winner.

> Twenty years from now you will be more disappointed by the things that you didn't do than by the ones you did do.
>
> —MARK TWAIN

Griffin accepted the honor wearing his Superman socks...cape (on the socks) and all. The junior quarterback known as RG3 flashed his wide smile when the winning announcement was made and made his way to the podium. "This is unbelievably believable," he said. "It's unbelievable because in the moment we're all amazed when great things happen. But it's believable because great things don't happen without hard work."

Griffin's comment unveiled a heavy dose of practical

philosophy for anyone passionate about becoming an expert.

Consider this--competence breeds confidence. Choose one area of your job. Commit yourself to becoming better at it than anyone else. Find an area in your life you have an interest in and master it.

To feel valued, to know even if only periodically, that you can do something better than anyone else can is an absolutely marvelous feeling.

David Casstevens of the *Dallas Morning News* told a great story about Frank Szymanski, a Notre Dame center in the 1940s. Frank was called to be a witness in a civil suit in South Bend.

"Are you on the Notre Dame Football team this year?" the judge asked.

"Yes, your Honor."

"What position?"

"Center, your Honor."

"How good a center?"

Szymanski squirmed a bit in his seat, but replied firmly, "Sir, I'm the best center Notre Dame has ever had."

Coach Frank Leahy, who was in the courtroom, was surprised at Szymanski's response. He had always been so modest and

> If you are called to be a street sweeper, sweep streets even as Michelangelo painted, or Beethoven composed music, or Shakespeare wrote poetry. Sweep streets so well that all the hosts of heaven and earth will pause to say, here lived a great street sweeper who did his job well.
>
> —MARTIN LUTHER KING, JR.

unassuming. So when the proceedings were over, he took Szymanski aside and asked why he had made such a statement. Szymanski blushed.

"I hated to do it, Coach," he said. "But, after all, I **was** under oath."

If you were under oath, what testimony would you be able to give about your professional competence? Do you have a burning desire to master what you do and be considered the best?

Rosalynn Carter's comment makes good sense, "If you doubt you can accomplish something, then you can't accomplish it. You have to have the confidence in your ability and then be tough enough to follow through." Learn what it takes to become your best. Have the courage to follow through. Invest yourself totally in becoming better than anyone ever thought you could, including yourself.

> Getting ahead in a difficult profession requires avid faith in yourself. That is why some people with mediocre talent, but with the inner drive, go much farther than people with vastly superior talent.
> —SOPHIA LOREN

Time. Commitment. Energy. Passion. Practice. Make them your friends.

Become an expert at what you do.

CHAPTER 2

SIMPLE SUCCESS STRATEGIES

VIVIDLY RECALL THE White Rabbit in *Alice's Adventures* in Wonderland. He was always racing here and there, talking nonstop about how late he was and yet making very little progress. Well, as I watch people today, it seems we've all become White Rabbits, dashing around trying to do more in less time; mindful of the impact this lifestyle has but doing little to remedy the situation.

People who achieve substantial success are often perceived as being big dreamers, creative thinkers, expert planners and most of all, consummate doers. There are some added simple principles critical for sustained success. **First, success comes from small efforts hammered out day by day.** People often sabotage their success by believing some grandiose achievement is necessary to determine whether or not they are successful.

It's imperative that you be happy right where you are with what you have while pursuing what you want. Then, success can follow.

"I couldn't wait for success," declared Jonathan Winters, "so I went on ahead without it." So did Drew Carey.

Comedian Drew Carey certainly didn't grow up in a

culture that molded his sense of humor. Carey was only eight when his father died and a year later he was molested. Life didn't get easier. As a college student at Kent State, he attempted suicide at a fraternity party, struggled to achieve acceptable grades and ultimately left after five years without a degree.

Carey became a drifter and once again attempted suicide. He then began reading, learning and applying principles for taking responsibility for his life. Then, a friend asked him to write jokes for a comedy show. Next thing you know he's on stage at a comedy club. *Star Search* and *The Tonight Show* followed, after which his success snowballed.

> Success is waking up in the morning, whoever you are, wherever you are, however old or young, and bounding out of bed because there's something out there that you love to do, that you believe in, that you're good at -something that's bigger than you are, and you can hardly wait to get at it again today.
> —WHIT HOBBS

Coping, drifting, irresponsibility, 'settling', compromise: these are not the steps to success. Begin conceptualizing and molding your success one small step at a time.

My second success observation - **Pleasure precedes success.**

That's Right! Your chances for success in any undertaking can be measured by the degree of pleasure you feel in what you do.

If what you're doing today is not satisfying, fulfilling,

gratifying...you're not successful. Chances are you feel stress day in and day out. Make a change.

Marcus Buckingham, writing in his book, *The One Thing You Need To Know*, advises: "The one thing you need to know about sustained individual success: Discover what you don't like doing and stop doing it."

Interestingly enough, successful people are often quitters. They quit doing things they abhor to free up their time and talents to excel at something that engages and energizes them.

Best-selling author Michael Crichton certainly understands this success principle. Crichton graduated from Harvard Medical School and completed a postdoctoral fellowship at the prestigious SALK Institute for Biological Studies; certainly guaranteeing him a successful and lucrative career as a doctor or as a medical researcher. But what was deemed a successful career by his family and colleagues was stressful to Michael Crichton.

Understanding pleasure precedes success, Crichton traded a secure future for an unpredictable writing career. Crichton concluded he didn't have the stomach for cutting people open or a passion for the medical field...regardless of the money, prestige, or perceived success it would bring.

Beware the tendency to underestimate your success because you are simply doing what you find pleasure in doing. Doing what you love to do is the epitome of success.

"To succeed," suggested Tony Dorsett, "you need to

find something to hold on to, something to motivate you, something to inspire you."

Number three. **Success breeds success.** (Told you these were simple.)

Have you ever noticed how a little success fuels energy, arouses desire, increases motivation; which breeds more success, elevates drive, fuels ambition, creates more dreams and the success cycle continues.

Out of incredible commitment, unwavering determination, and hard work combined with God given ability success breeds success.

Wayne Gretzky owns roughly 60 records, is a 10-time scoring champion and a nine-time MVP. "I was a boy that happened to love a game and got lucky," said Gretzky in an interview, "and the good Lord gave me a passion for it."

> The grass may look greener on the other side, but it still has to be mowed.
>
> —B.C. FORBES

Think about it—focused effort, combined with the pleasure of doing what we do, creates success that tends to reproduce itself. Pretty simple – but powerful!

Another "love it" strategy is to **focus on people. Become a Picker-Upper-Person**.

"It's All About Relationships!" I frequently use that phrase in meetings, one-to-one conversations, social situations and yes, even airplanes. Brian Tracy believes, "85% of our job happiness in life comes from our interaction with others."

Who are Picker-Upper People? Consider the following characteristics that positively impact people's lives. Maybe there is one or two you could work on refining in your life.

- Accept people unconditionally. Accept people for who they are; not what they could be if only they listened to you.
- Seek to understand life from the other person's perspective. Get inside their world.
- Listen with sincerity and an open mind. Learn from others. Show genuine interest in other people's lives. Talk less. Leave your ego at the door.
- Respect what is important or valued by others. Respect other's opinions.
- Be enjoyable to be around. Kind. Gracious. Polite. Tactful. Don't get uptight by little things that bother you. Make it possible for people to say, "I like myself better when I'm with you."
- Refrain from criticism. Overlook people's faults. Overlook minor or petty differences.
- Cherish conflict – momentarily. Quickly and sincerely attempt to resolve any conflict.
- Freely provide recognition and appreciation. Go to great lengths to make people feel appreciated.

- Get excited about other people's success. Congratulate them. Share in their exuberance. Be their best cheerleader and promoter.

Here's a relationship jump start. For the next 30 days, treat everyone you come in contact with as the most important person in your life. Place every greeting, phone call, interaction and goodbye with a heightened level of respect.

Everyone you encounter wants to be important to someone, to be loved, respected and considered special. It could very well be you were placed in their life at this moment in time to add value and significance. What a great opportunity!

There is a side benefit to this approach. People who make treating others as the most important people in their life often find that others begin treating them the same way. It's funny how life tends to give us back what we give. One thing is for sure, those you touch will not remain as they are – and I doubt you will either.

Ironically, when I unselfishly brighten another person's world, my world becomes a bit brighter. Who needs you to show a measure of concern? What are the strengths of your co-workers? Show kindness to someone who is unable to return your gesture. Give up fifteen minutes in your day to build a better relationship with one person. You get the idea.

If you are feeling a little disheartened about your life or job, find a way to enrich the life of someone else. You'll be amazed at the result. Give it a try.

Finally, stretch yourself. Heighten your personal expectations. Challenge the walls of your current responsibilities. Be imaginative. Confront the status quo and take responsibility to work toward achievements uncommon to your position. Choose to make a difference. Dig in and find a way to produce the unexpected.

You may feel you have reached the point where you want to "take this job and shove it." It's not energizing and inspiring you like you want. Consider your options:

1. Do absolutely nothing and hope for a magical intervention by the tooth fairy.

2. Leave your position so you don't suck the energy out of other people.

3. Take some time to consider what you could do to transform your current job into something you would enjoy.

4. Figure out what your ideal job is and create it or go find it.

If you think the grass looks greener on the other side of the fence, it might be because someone is fertilizing it. I'm sure the water bill is higher there as well. The perfect lawn doesn't just happen.

Neither does the perfect job.

Francis Ford Coppola once said, "If you love something, you'll bring so much of yourself to it that it will create your future." People who love what they do invest their heart, mind and spirit into everything they do. They are totally immersed and invested in what they are doing. How do you get there? Explore some new ways of thinking and approaching your job.

> Are you bored with life? Then throw yourself into some work you believe in with all your heart, live for it, die for it, and you will find happiness that you had thought could never be yours.
> —DALE CARNEGIE

Do yourself a favor and throw yourself wholeheartedly into becoming a master at what you do. Work as hard as you can to be the best you can be at what you choose to do.

Take it from Reggie Leach: "Success is not the result of spontaneous combustion. You must set yourself on fire."

CHAPTER 3

THE MODEL EMPLOYEE

W<small>HAT DOES THE</small> model employee look like, act like, perform like, and behave like?

Several years ago, a Sheriff's Deputy traveled to Northern Minnesota to pick up a prisoner at a minimum security prison. Upon checking in at the hotel he asked the clerk what they did for fun and excitement in their community.

"In the evenings," he responded, "we go down to the lake and watch the moose dance on ice. It's delightful."

The deputy decided experiencing this strange activity was better than nothing or staring at the walls in his hotel room. Checking out of the hotel the next morning, the deputy let the clerk know he went down to the lake the night before to watch the moose dance on the ice. "It was the worst thing I ever saw," he told the clerk. "The animals were clumsy and uncoordinated. They were falling all over themselves and the ice."

"Well, of course they were," sneered the local. "No one goes to the lake on Wednesday. That's amateur night."

Today's team member can't afford to act like an amateur. Regardless of the day or the situation, organizations need our best effort every minute of every day. Model employees understand the necessity to take their performance to a heightened level. There are significant distinctions between remarkable employees and the amateur (good employees). Here are a few distinguishing qualities.

Love What They Do. Model employees do what they love and love what they do. As Billy Cox indicated, "If you don't love what you do, you have two choices. You can either change what you're doing or you can change what you love." Loving what you do is fundamental to becoming a team member with exceptional value. I don't mean 'like your job.' I'm talking about an unmatched, irrepressible, intoxicating passion for what you do. Only those who have it understand it. Others find it just a bit strange…almost irritating. It's okay to be a bit quirky --- passionate about what you do.

Exceed Expectations. Exceptional employees could care less about their job description. They are motivated by doing whatever it takes to generate results to help their organization succeed. In fact, their mantra is do whatever it takes and then just 'a little bit more.' Regardless of the job expectations, the model employee understands the job description is a minimal guide for their daily contribution. They have higher aspirations. They transform the ordinary into the extraordinary.

Make Relationships a Priority. Ben Stein got my attention when he said, "Personal relationships are the fertile soil from which all advancement, all success, all achievement in real life grows." Note the use of the word "all."

Remember the Academy Award winning movie *Rocky*? I love the scene where boxer Rocky Balboa describes his relationship with his girlfriend, Adrian: "I've got gaps. She's got gaps. But together we've got no gaps." Collaborative relationships minimize, or even eliminate the gaps.

Work Smart. Model employees zealously refrain from committing random acts of stupidity. They don't do dumb things. Notably, they don't shoot themselves in the foot by taking action that causes others to say, "What was that all about?"

Be a Problem Solver. As John Maxwell said, "Many people would rather deal with old problems than find new solutions." Not true of the truly outstanding employee. Peter Drucker once commented that; "People do not want to hear about your labor pains. They want to see the baby."

The mediocre, normal, run of the mill team member tends to talk about their problems, dwell on them and sometimes even exaggerate their problems. The model employee produces results despite their challenges and sometimes because of their problems.

Devoted to Excellence. Mediocre or good enough is never in the vocabulary of an outstanding employee. They are always tinkering, massaging, fooling around, or experimenting to create excellence. Other people love policies and procedures while the model employee loves to find a better way.

If you want to be average, do what average people are doing. Excellence happens when you think about it, talk about it, and model it all day long, every day. Such is the *modus operandi* of the model employee.

WHAT HAPPENS IN THE BREAK ROOM STAYS IN THE BREAK ROOM

I am not a fan of the Las Vegas motto that 'what happens in Vegas, stays in Vegas.' My moral make-up suggests this promotion is an excuse to do whatever you want without personal, moral, emotional, etc. responsibility or ramifications. Scary!

(Maybe the motto should read: 'what happens in Vegas...shouldn't.')

Let's take a little different slant as it relates to being a professional. How about this: "What happens in the break room...stays in the break room?"

When you arrive at work, finish your break, or are done with lunch, imagine opening the door to a thousand screaming fans anxiously awaiting your command performance. It's time to give it your best shot. The fans deserve it. Your fellow performers are depending on you to help them look good. And the director is depending on you to use your unique talent to make the production a success. As you can see, your job is bigger than the tasks you perform. There are people depending on you.

Perform your best and the accolades are sure to come. Behave unprofessionally, and you're bound to have a short career. Leave anything that detracts from your ability to perform behind that imaginary closed door.

Do you have an attitude about something that happened on your shift yesterday? Or just an "attitude" in general? Is there an irritating conflict between you and another team member? Is there anything about you today that would be offensive to those you serve? Did you leave your smile backstage, or have you lost it completely? Have you complained about a team member to someone else?

I'm sure you can think of a number of examples that serve as a detour to *being professional*. The key question in my mind is: "Is my behavior and attitude reflecting the demeanor of one who is truly *being professional*? Everything we do, say, or think is an expression of our level of commitment to excellence and our desire to be professional.

The more I think of it, how about changing the thinking to, "What happens in the parking lot, stays in the parking lot"?

Let's not allow the unprofessional behavior to leak anywhere into our work environment. "Park it" in the parking lot. That way we can make the break room our staging room, encouragement center, relationship development area and a space where teams can share their ideas for making their professional lives better.

Under the pressure of our day-to-day demands, our standards can easily become sidelined or left in the parking lot. Consistently *being professional* surfaces when professional behaviors, actions and attitudes become second nature, a way of life, part of our DNA.

What do I need to do to perform my best today? What do I need to leave in the parking lot?

This certainly isn't an exhaustive list of a remarkable professional's characteristics, but it's a great start. Once I get these qualities mastered, I'm sure I'll discover another set of admirable qualities to pursue.

CHAPTER 4

ATTITUDE CHECK

A MAN JOINED A monastery of Trappist monks, where, in addition to the vows of celibacy and poverty, he was required to take a vow of silence. The Monastery allowed him to speak two words a year.

At the conclusion of his first year, he was asked by his superiors what he had to say. The amateur monk responded, "Food cold!"

He was thanked for his comments and the man retreated for another year of prayer and meditation.

Two years after his arrival, the aspiring monk was once again escorted to his senior monk who greeted him and asked what he would like to share this year.

The man replied, "Bed hard!"

Once again, he reentered his silent world.

Healthy people go 'Yes,' 'No,' and 'Whoopee.' Unhealthy people go 'Yes, but,' 'No, but,' and 'No whoopee!'
—ERIC BERNE

By the end of the third year, the monk was familiar with the process. He made his way into the meditative quarters of his superiors who repeated the anticipated process.

"It has been three years, what is on your mind this year?"

The man adamantly responded, "I Quit!"

His superior responded, "Your decision doesn't surprise us; after all, for the last three years you've done nothing but complain."

Let it be known the world is full of people who complain, complain, complain. You probably already knew that. Nothing can cause more widespread stress in the work place than a chronic complainer.

I recently heard about a group of people who, over a few years, resigned, retired or were released from the same employer. They still gather periodically for 'happy hour' to complain about their past employer and relive their unhappiness. Apparently they subscribe to Drew Carey's observation: "Oh, you hate your job? Why didn't you say so? There's a support group for that. It's called everybody, and they meet at the bar." Yikes! Doesn't seem like a good antibiotic for healing the nagging infection of being disgruntled.

I learned a long time ago from Lou Holtz that, "The man who complains about the way the ball bounces is likely the one who dropped it."*

So what's my point? Stay away from these compulsive complaining people. Limit your exposure to their 'life is terrible' addiction. They will suck the energy from your very body. Unfortunately, there is no transfusion available to replenish the lost vitality, but separation will help.

---

* http://quotationsbook.com/quote/7608/

Even more important, don't be one of these people. Beware! Most complainers don't think or know they are energy suckers.

So what is the alternative attitude? Find something good about your job, the people you work with, the lunch hour they provide, the paycheck you receive...Something! Dwell on it until you get your mind off of the negative. If nothing else, at least spend equal time in gratitude as you do complaining.

> To one man, the world is barren, dull, and superficial; to another, rich, interesting, and full of meaning.
> —ARTHUR SCHOPENHAUER

Stay away from the 'poor me' mentality. Other people are just as busy as you are, have as many or more problems as you do and don't have the energy to heal your life and theirs. If only we all spent as much time being thankful for the blessings we receive as we do the bummers we experience.

Do a little self-analysis concerning your complaining quotient. Ask a trusted friend what they think of your attitude. Tell a trusted friend, co-worker or neighbor you can no longer endure exposure to their continual complaining. You'll be amazed at the renewed vigor you will experience at every ounce of negativity you shed...yours and others.

Once you rid yourself of complaining, it's imperative to understand that everything starts inside of you. You create the world you want to live in. Paul Cousins said, "How things look on the outside of us depends on how things are on the inside of us." The world mirrors back to us the reflection of our attitudes.

I don't know why it is so difficult to get people to see the tremendous damage they do to themselves by walking around with a chip on their shoulder and a continual black cloud in their outlook. If only we could get them to understand Groucho Marx's conviction that, "I, not events, have the power to make me happy or unhappy today. I can choose which it shall be. Yesterday is dead, tomorrow hasn't arrived yet. I have just one day, today, and I'm going to be happy in it."

> Totally self-responsible people look upon themselves as self-employed... no matter who signs their paychecks, in the final analysis they work for themselves.
> —BRIAN TRACY

I became convinced many years ago that negative people simply make difficulties out of every opportunity. Positive people look for the opportunities in every difficulty. How do they do it? Through disciplined behavior that generates the power to live optimistically. They have a realistic view of life but always maintain their right to choose how they respond. They say, think, and do things that perpetuate their optimism.

Positive people nurture positive habits and eliminate the destructive aspects of their lifestyle. Looking for the good in other people reinforces the good that is within themselves and their experiences. They look to the future with positive anticipation and realize they may not be able to change the world they see around them, but they can certainly change the way they see the world within. They literally stop themselves when negative conversations begin to flow through their lips and finish what they had to say in an upbeat way.

You can control your attitude. You can be more positive. You can be in a good mood. You can weed out the negativity that surrounds you. Learning to live with a bright view of your life, the world, and your future is a wonderful gift and one that you can give to yourself.

Become a **Yes, I Can** Person.

You know those people who only feel good when they feel bad; they only have something to say when it is negative or are only happy when they are unhappy. They are all around us.

I prefer to emulate the attitude and spirit displayed in this story. In his book *Go For The Magic*, Pat Williams recounts a story told by St. Louis sportswriter Bob Broeg about baseball Hall of Fame player Stan Musial, who was known as one of the game's most consistent players.

One day when Musial was playing for the St. Louis Cardinals, a teammate came into the clubhouse whistling. He turned to Stan and said, "I feel great. My home life is happy. I'm in a groove. I feel like I'm going to get two hits today. Ever feel like that, Stan?"

Smiling, Musial looked at him and said, "Every day!"

We all know that anyone, no matter how good the circumstances are, can find a reason to have a negative attitude. And everyone, no matter how bad the circumstances are, can find a way to maintain a good attitude. It is simply a choice!

One of my favorite authors, Chuck Swindoll, explains in his book, *Laugh Again,* that when Mother Teresa was asked the requirements for people assisting in her work with the destitute in Calcutta, she cited two things:

1. the desire to work hard
2. a joyful attitude

If someone could be expected to be joyful among the dying and the poorest of the poor, then certainly we can do the same in our situation.

Several things on a team are not contagious. Talent. Experience. Willingness to practice. But we can be sure of one thing: Attitude is catching. What does a "Yes, I Can" person look like? They. . .

- Possess an unwavering passion for what they do
- Love what they do
- Have a high energy level
- Display a "How can I make it happen?" mentality
- Never use the words – "It's not my job."
- Always look for a better way
- Look for the best in every situation

- Leave every situation better than they found it

"Yes, I Can" people display a visual love for what they do which generates passion and sustains a high energy level. "Yes, I Can" people never worry about burning out. They are more concerned about rusting out.

No matter how small or large the task, "Yes I Can" people pitch in. Try it for a week. Approach every situation with a "Yes, I Can" mentality.

> Wake up with a smile and go after life.... Live it, enjoy it, taste it, smell it, feel it.
> —JOE KNAPP

Dr. William Glasser maintained, "If you want to change attitudes, start with a change in behavior. In other words, begin to act the part, as well as you can, of the person you would rather be, the person you most want to become. Gradually, the old, fearful person will fade away." Give it a try. See if a heightened sense of expectations and behaviors result.

When you determine to stop complaining or trying to be someone else, you can focus on what you do best and go after your professional life with a smile on your face every morning!

CHAPTER 5

ROW, ROW, ROW YOUR BOAT— NOT SOMEONE ELSE'S

E VERY DAY, PEOPLE are involved in jobs they don't enjoy. Still others are engrossed in careers they don't want. Work becomes an irritating necessity that strips them of professional fulfillment and satisfaction.

Remember as children how we sang over and over again the words of the famous song *Row, Row, Row Your Boat*? Let me refresh your memory:

Row, row, row your boat
Gently down the stream
Merrily, merrily, merrily, merrily
Life is but a dream.

These lyrics contain a powerful message. Row, row, row whose boat? That's right—YOUR boat. Not someone else's boat or the boat someone told you to row. What boat (career) do you want to be in? Quite simply, if you hate music, then playing in the orchestra will not make work a dream. A nightmare would be more like it. What do you enjoy most? In an ideal world, where would you like to be in your career?

Tap Into the Power of Your Potential

Before you man the oars of your own boat, you need to know where you are capable of going. And don't underestimate yourself! Denis Waitley challenges me when he says, "Never rest on your achievements; always nurture your potential." How does that apply to me? What is my potential?

> If you don't love what you do, you have two choices. You can either change what you're doing or you can change what you love.
>
> —Billy Wilcox

City slicker Smith smiled as he exited the hardware store with his brand new power chainsaw. Guaranteed to cut down several trees an hour, this was his ticket to clearing land on his new country acreage. Two days later, he returned to the store in a fit of frustration and anger. "This saw isn't worth a plug nickel. You guaranteed me it would cut down several trees an hour. I barely fell one tree in an entire day."

Somewhat puzzled, the store manager stepped outside with the saw, flipped the switch, and gave the cord a rip. The saw fired up and the steel-toothed chain whirled around the 24" guide bar. Startled by the deafening noise, Smith jumped back. "What's that noise?" he gasped.

Smith's failure to use the saw's built in power is similar to our common approach to getting more done. Limits are set on our achievement potential because we underestimate our capabilities. People sincerely believe they are just too busy to do more than their present output. They are only capable of cutting one tree per day. Yet, compared to what we are capable of, our horsepower may be functioning at only half or three-fourths its potential.

Countless intelligent people limit their life-enhancing, achievement-producing potential. They never move further than the boundaries of their self-imposed limitations or bountiful excuses. As scientist Willis R. Whitney pointed out, "Some men have thousands of reasons why they cannot do what they want to, when all they need is one reason why they can."

> Life is like a ten-speed bicycle. Most of us have gears we have never used.
>
> —LINUS, PEANUTS COMIC STRIP

I'm attempting to align myself with Erma Bombeck's desire that, "When I stand before God at the end of my life, I would hope that I would not have a single bit of talent left and could say, 'I used everything you gave me.'"

Winners are people who do not leave to chance the gift of time or opportunity to achieve. They realize they are not yet everything they are intended to be -- even though some of us have come farther than we ever thought we would. They pursue it systematically through the use of simple, fundamental truths that generate a new world of opportunity.

"A sobering thought," pondered Jane Wagner, "what if, right at this very moment, I am living up to my full potential?" I sincerely doubt that it is ever possible or we would need to redefine potential. In fact, Stanford research indicates we use less than 5 percent of our mental ability.

Be bold enough to envision and create a level of effectiveness beyond your present scope of thinking. You are intended to be a different person next month than you are today. There are accomplishments out there for you to encounter that haven't even entered your mind. You have potential power that is waiting to have its engine started.

"The only reason you are not the person you should be is because you don't dare to be," said William H. Danforth. "Once you dare, new powers harness themselves for your service."

Consider the advice of St. Francis of Assisi: "Start by doing what's necessary, then what's possible, and suddenly you are doing the impossible." What a great way to reveal the dormant, unused, untapped potential that exists within.

What do you 'dare' to become?

"Each one of us has some kind of vocation," said Thomas Merton. "We are called by God to share in His life and in His kingdom. Each one of us is called to a special place in the kingdom. If we find that place, we will be happy. If we do not find it, we can never be completely happy."

Do you love your vocation? Do you go home from work feeling fulfilled and satisfied? Do you begin each day looking forward to the challenges awaiting you? Is there a sense of peace about this being the job you were specifically chosen to do?

If you answer "yes" to these questions, the chances are

good you are rowing your boat, doing what you choose and love to do. If, on the other hand, you immediately answered "no," I assure you, a better fit between you and what you do is possible.

Be authentic!

In an effort to get all you can, remember that what you do to be successful is far less important than knowing and being who you are. Authenticity will allow you to begin your journey to greatness. Refrain from artificial ingredients that camouflage the real you.

A modern day model of authenticity is Dolly Parton. In *Parade* magazine, she said, "People who know me know that beneath these big boobs is a big heart, and beneath this big hair is a big brain. Over time, people see me as a real person and stop staring at the anatomy." Dolly Parton understands the obstacles she must overcome for people to see the real her. She is keenly aware that no matter what she achieves with her life, living her life consistent with who she really is will be the true measure of success.

> The easiest thing to be in the world is you. The most difficult thing to be is what other people want you to be. Don't let them put you in that position.
> —LEO BUSCAGLIA

Over time, people value the person who knows who they are and respects themselves for what they are. Be a genuine version of you.

Find your passion. Clarify what's important to you. Tap into your potential. Be authentic. Never mind attempting to be like someone else. Know who you are and what you have a burning desire to do. Move in the direction of your niche and enjoy the journey as much as the ultimate destination. Begin rowing YOUR boat today and experience the achievement and satisfaction reserved for you.

CHAPTER 6

FOCUS ON WHAT YOU DO BEST!

MANY OF US may aspire to lead a life like someone else. I wonder what life would be like as a tall, handsome and dashing movie star, professional golfer, airline pilot or even the president.

Malcolm Forbes once said, "Too many people overvalue what they are not and undervalue what they are." How true. Isn't it amazing how we tend to compare ourselves with something other than who we are? Comparing what you are to what you think you should be or acting like someone you're not is a losing battle.

In his youth, John Philip Sousa, the grandson of America's great composer and conductor by the same name, received large sums of money by appearing as a guest bandleader. After a period of masquerading, his conscience began eating away at him. He knew he was asked to guest conduct because of his famous grandfather, not due to his own musical ability. In fact, the young maestro couldn't read a note of music. He

> Beware of no one more than yourself; we carry our worst enemies within us.
> —CHARLES SPURGEON

soon gave up his lucrative charade and started working for a living.

One of the qualities people admire in former First Lady Barbara Bush is her acceptance of herself as she is. Comparing herself to her predecessor, the First Lady said, "Nancy Reagan adores her husband; I adore mine. She fights drugs; I fight illiteracy. She wears a size 3; so is my leg."

No apologies. No should-ofs, would-ofs or could-ofs. Just a healthy acceptance of who she is. Mrs. Bush possesses a healthy self-love. She respects herself based on a proper perspective of who she is.

That healthy, non-apologetic attitude allowed Mrs. Bush to make the most of who she is. She doesn't spend her time trying to be like someone else or acting in a manner inconsistent with the way she sees herself. When you love and accept yourself for who you are, you have nothing left to prove. Being who you are makes it possible for you to become better than you are.

As a little boy, he was unusually shy and noticeably thin. He wanted to be a tough guy, but no matter what he ate, he couldn't gain a pound. To make matter's worse, he was a minister's son, and that certainly didn't make him popular. The other members of his family were outgoing and endowed with public speaking ability. He wanted nothing to do with that kind of responsibility.

"I was shy and bashful," he says, "and this self-image of inadequacy might have gone on indefinitely had it not been for something a professor said to me during my sophomore year in college. One day, after I made a miserable showing, he told me to wait after class. 'How long are you going to be bashful like this, a scared rabbit afraid of the sound of your voice?' he demanded. 'You'd better change the way you think about yourself, Peale, before it's too late.'"

Norman Vincent Peale went on to become a world renowned speaker and author. The talent he possessed laid dormant because he was investing more time and energy dwelling on what he couldn't do than exposing what he was capable of.

In his book, *Making The Most of Life*, J.R. Miller told a heart-warming story about Leonardo da Vinci. While da Vinci was still a student, long before he became a renowned renaissance artist, his old and famous teacher asked him to finish a picture he had begun. The young student was in such awe of his teacher's talent that he initially declined the request. His instructor would not accept no for an answer and handed da Vinci the brush, along with these encouraging words: "Do your best."

DaVinci took the brush and his trembling hands began to stroke the canvas. He gradually gained confidence, his hand grew steady, and his eye "awoke with slumbering genius." Soon he overcame his initial timidity and found himself engrossed in his work. When the painting was finished, the master teacher was brought into the studio to see it. Filled with pride over his student's achievement, he embraced da Vinci and exclaimed, "My son, I paint no more!"

Leonardo da Vinci was a common person with an undeveloped talent. He became a master of his trade when he continually did the best with what he had. Henry Van Dyke once suggested, "Use that talent you possess; the woods would be very silent if no birds sang there except those that sang best."

Da Vinci's instructor had a keen sense of talent and an even wiser approach to surfacing talent in order to maximize da Vinci's potential. As Peter Drucker believed, "To build on a person's strengths, that is, to enable him to do what he can do, will make him effective...to try to build on his weaknesses will be...frustrating and stultifying."

What talents have you been timid with? What undeveloped abilities do you possess that are just waiting to blossom? Like Leonardo, your true abilities will surface when you do the best with what you have.

Start viewing yourself as a bundle of potential waiting to be opened - not a package of limitations.

See yourself as endowed with a unique selection of talents, abilities and skills - not as one left with an empty bag when talents were distributed.

Begin seeing yourself as a person with an exciting future of successes, enjoyment, and opportunities to use what you're good at.

Your self image rises when you use the gifts you've been given. Get started on your list.

WHAT DO YOU DO BEST?

I love the story of the ninety-year-old man who, when asked if he knew how to play golf, responded that he didn't know. "What do you mean, you don't know?" he was asked. The man, with a wry grin on his face, replied, "I've never tried."

Many of us have talents, abilities and gifts we've never fully developed. Others haven't taken the time to identify their strengths and still others don't have a clue what they can do because they've never tried.

> My mother said to me, "If you become a soldier, you'll be a general; if you become a monk you'll end up as the pope." Instead, I became a painter and wound up as Picasso.
> —PABLO PICASSO

Gallup, Inc., an international research and consulting company, studied 250,000 successful people and concluded that "the highest levels of personal achievement came when people matched their activities with their strengths."

Author H. Jackson Brown Jr. quipped, "Talent without discipline is like an octopus on roller skates. There's plenty of movement, but you never know if it's going to be forward, backward, or sideways." If you know you have talent, and you've seen a lot of motion – but little concrete results - you might benefit from an intense strengths focus.

Activity without productivity is often talent without disciplined application. We have a responsibility to nurture our talents to become the best we can be so we are prepared for life's opportunities. But how? How do I develop the necessary discipline to develop my natural abilities? Actually, it's simpler than you might think.

First, determine what you are naturally good at. What activities tend to give you a natural high, peak your interest, or trip your trigger? Where do you enjoy investing yourself? What comes easily to you? What tasks are a no-brainer for you to accomplish?

Secondly, find a way to invest yourself enlarging your talents. Professionals understand the price to be paid to achieve impressive results. They practice, apply and refine their talent. Find paths to contributing your unique abilities to achieve what your organization needs you to do and produce uncommon results.

> When I stand before God at the end of my life, I would hope that I would not have a single bit of talent left, and could say, "I used everything you gave me.
>
> —ERMA BOMBECK

Follow the wisdom of basketball great Larry Bird. "A winner is someone who recognizes his God-given talents, works his tail off to develop them into skills, and uses those skills to accomplish his goals." This is a wonderful lead-in to our final step.

Finally, Act! Sitting on the sideline is unacceptable. What is holding you back? What keeps you from applying your God-given abilities? Face it head on. It is time to do what you were designed to do. Find a need and invest everything you have in making life better for someone else.

Are you using your power? Are you doing all God equipped you to do? Have you joined the anti-just-get-by league? Commit fully to the power that is in you. I love what Charles Swindoll says about having the discipline to apply ourselves. "When you do the most what you do the best," he said, "you put a smile on God's face. What could be better than that?"

Don't paint stripes on your back if you're not a zebra. Focus on building upon your unique abilities.

—LEE J. COLAN

CHAPTER 7

YOUR LIFE HAS TO PROVE IT!

WHAT IS THE difference between the person people think you are and who you really are? What is your reputation? Is it an accurate reflection of the real you?

In 2009, Tiger Wood's career, as well as personal and public image, was decimated. Running his SUV into a fire hydrant Thanksgiving weekend was only the beginning of the crashes he would experience. His infidelities became public and a critical eye watched his every move. A massive scandal ended his marriage and stripped Tiger of the respect he had earned from his fans.

Twenty nine months after being dethroned as the #1 player in the world, Tiger Woods returned to the helm. But, the baggage he carried in the public's eye hasn't necessarily returned him to a #1 rating in the public's heart.

Enron, Bernie Madhoff, Lance Armstrong, John Edwards – you get the idea – should understand the power of character.

Nathaniel Hawthorne declared, "No man can for any considerable time, wear one face to himself and another to the multitude without finally getting bewildered as to which is the true one."

Certainly, a good reputation is a worthy pursuit. It is important, however, to understand that your character will ultimately determine the reputation you attain.

Character tells people how you are put together. It is a simultaneous display of beliefs and actions. Character allows you to be authentic, while developing the reputation you aspire to achieve. Above all, character allows you to be you. There is no need for facades, putting on an act, or fearing your true self will be found out. People with character can be transparent. When character is a reflection of your inner values, the outcome will be a respectable reputation.

> Be more concerned with your character than your reputation, because your character is what you really are, while your reputation is merely what others think you are.
>
> —JOHN WOODEN

Character is all about the little things in our lives. It is developed in the moments when we don't have time to think, but act according to our beliefs. It is revealed in how we respond to people no matter what their status.

Character is who you are when no one is looking. A solid character remains consistent no matter where you are, who you are with, and in whatever situations you encounter. Who surfaces in these scenarios is the genuine, actual you.

Character remains firmly grounded in the best of

times and the worst. Character driven people take full responsibility for their lives. They are willing to say, "I'm sorry" and readily admit when they are wrong. Ego is set aside. A serving attitude is firmly in place.

Our public image is what people think we are. Character is what we really are. Pay attention to the authentic you.

Character takes responsibility seriously. When you consciously take responsibility for the outcomes in your life, new possibilities and alternatives will surface. Responsible people see no reason to blame others or the world around them for how they feel, think, or act. A person of character will face the facts, meet challenges, decide how to make changes, and actively plan how they will make a difference in their future.

> If you're tough on yourself, life is going to be infinitely easier on you.
> —Zig Ziglar

Our character and integrity are inseparable. Billy Graham was once quoted as saying, "Integrity is the glue that holds our life together." In addition, it is fair to say that integrity is a primary ingredient that gives others a glimpse of our character.

In the late 1960s, my mother worked for J.C. Penney's in Sioux Falls, South Dakota. I loved going to visit her at work because they had the city's only escalator and I could be easily entertained just riding up and down the escalator (Remember, this was the '60s). To this day, I remember my mother's infatuation with Penney's reputation. He was a man of integrity.

In his book, *View from the Ninth Decade*, J.C. Penney tells of working at the local grocer as a young boy and telling his father how the owner would mix two grades of coffee and sell the mixture at a higher price. Young Penney thought the village grocer was quite innovative, but his father pointed out that this little trick was dishonest. He made the point so strongly that young Penney quit his job. From that day forward, Penney made honesty and integrity the foundation of his decisions, actions and business practices throughout his lifetime.

J.C. Penney's high moral principles, business ethics and passion for maintaining the highest reputation impressed my mother...and millions of employees and customers throughout the years.

Television commentator Ted Koppel says, "There's harmony and inner peace to be found in following a moral compass that points in the same direction regardless of fashion or trend."

People should feel at ease and comfortable with the way we do things. They should never feel the need to question either our motives or our actions. Everyone knows beyond a shadow of a doubt that we will do what we say and be who we claim to be. We deliver on our commitments. No exceptions. It's our moral compass. And yes, it proves our character.

As I write this, our company's owner and I are stranded

by a weather delay in the Washington, D.C. airport waiting to catch a flight home. It's getting late, but we are reservedly optimistic that we will be on that last plane home. Jack is working his Sudoku puzzles, but I couldn't resist interrupting to get his input to this question, "If you could tell 3,500 staff in our company how to be a person of integrity, what would you say?"

Here it is – "Your actions and words have to be consistent. People never have to wonder about you. They know what you believe. You do everything with fairness, honesty and compassion." Then,

> Real integrity is doing the right thing, knowing that nobody's going to know whether you did it or not.
> —OPRAH WINFREY

he got my attention, "You can say it, but your life has to prove it."

"Your life has to prove it!" Prove what? That you are willing to do the right thing, even if nobody notices or even if there is no chance you would be caught doing the wrong thing.

Here are a few thoughts for living a life that proves it.

1. Do What's Right

A young nurse landed her first surgical nurse position and was assisting a surgeon for the first time. As he was completing the operation, she told him he had used 12 sponges, but she could account for only 11. The doctor curtly replied that he had removed them all from inside the patient. The nurse insisted that one was missing, but the doctor disregarded her caution and indicated he would proceed with sewing up the incision.

The nurse, visibly upset, said, "You can't do that! Think of the patient!" The doctor smiled and, lifting his foot, revealed the twelfth sponge, which he had deliberately dropped on the floor. "You'll be a great surgical nurse!" he said. She had passed the integrity test.

Here's an opposite example. Remember the Challenger Space Shuttle incident in 1986 – if you're old enough. Engineers on that project knew the lowered temperatures could impact the O-rings; however, they believed they could not say anything without putting their jobs at risk. The culture of not telling the truth directly contributed to the loss of seven lives and put our space program in a downward spiral for years. Needless to say, a lack of integrity can have dramatic consequences. Do what's right.

2. Strengthen Your Trust Quotient

Write down the names of five people you trust. Choose anyone in your life who has proven themselves trustworthy. Go ahead, write them down:

1.

2.

3.

4.

5.

Review the list to make sure these are the most trustworthy people in your life. Ask yourself, "What characteristics do these people have in common?"

Now think of five people you do not trust. What traits do they share?

I'm willing to place a little wager that your trustworthy list includes people who possess a high level of integrity and moral aptitude. Of course, the characteristics of the people we don't trust aren't worth reinforcing. These are the people you learn a great deal from – on what NOT to do.

Here's the deal. You should be striving every minute of every day to get on people's "trust" list. What does that mean? It doesn't matter how great your attitude is, how competent you are or what skills you possess if people can't trust you.

Over the years, I've asked 1,000's of seminar participants to describe those people they trust. The common responses go something like this:

"I can depend on them."

"I know they want the best for me."

"I feel safe."

"Their motives are pure."

"They believe in me."

Now think about those people in your department with whom you would like a closer trusting relationship. Take the first step and determine what you can do to nurture that relationship.

3. Be Truthful In All Things

A man wrote this note to the Internal Revenue Service: "I have been unable to sleep knowing that I have cheated on my income tax. I understated my taxable income and have enclosed a check for $150. If I still can't sleep, I'll send the rest."

The best way to get a good night's sleep is to be honest while you're awake. Twelve-year-old Jimmy was a key witness in a highly public lawsuit. One of the lawyers, after intense questioning, asked, "Your father told you what to say, didn't he?"

"Yes," answered the boy.

"Now tell us," pursued the lawyer, "what were his instructions?"

"Well," replied the boy, "Father told me the lawyers would try to tangle me in my testimony, but if I would just be careful and tell the truth, I could say the same thing every time."

Mark Twain was reportedly once asked, "What's the difference between a liar and a person who tells the truth?" Twain promptly replied, "Very simple. A liar has to have a better memory."

Your life has to prove it and it's much easier when we do what's right and say what's right the first time.

4. Be the Real Deal

I love this expression I recently heard from a country preacher. "Be who you is, 'cause if you ain't who you is, you is who you ain't."

Intentions are wonderful. Optimism is admirable. Talents are desirable. Intellect is even nice to have. Unfortunately, none of these traits really matter if your integrity is uncertain. People with integrity possess a most admirable quality in this day and age of deception, dishonesty and disconnect between values and actions.

You've got to be the real deal.

As our Billionaire Omahan Warren Buffet said, "It takes 20 years to build a reputation and five minutes to ruin it. If you think about that, you'll do things differently."

CHAPTER 8

THE POWER OF TEAM SPIRIT

THE CONCEPT OF teamwork seems to be worn out. Maybe we've overused the term without fully understanding the intent, process or outcomes. Regardless, I'm well aware that lip service without practical application or personal commitment has bred indifference into this age old concept.

I'm beginning to lean more toward the idea of "team spirit." Legendary basketball coach John Wooden defines it as **"an eagerness to sacrifice personal interests and glory for the good and greatness of the team."** I love that definition.

What would happen if everyone on your team agreed to give up just one of their personal interests for the good of the team for 30 days? What if each person was willing to sacrifice personal achievement or satisfaction for the team's success? What if "we" rather than "me" guided all decisions for a month? I'm talking more than a token effort here. Let's think about a full-fledged selfless pursuit of team spirit.

Sound simple? Maybe. There are substantial egos, agendas, selfish interests, personal hang-ups and a host of other issues you'll have to contend with. Try it anyway. Challenge your team. The potential results are worth the required effort.

Let me illustrate. I'm normally glued to the Olympics. There's something about patriotism combined with watching sports I know very little about, cheering my heart out, celebrating the successes and grieving the losses. Personal and team success is undoubtedly magnified in this venue.

> The most important measure of how good a game I played was how much better I'd made my teammates play.
> —BILL RUSSELL, BOSTON CELTICS HALL OF FAME

Let's go back in time to the 2004 Summer Olympics in Athens. Michael Phelps was having a wonderfully successful Olympic experience. He was prepared for yet another event. His competition was favored teammate Ian Crocker who had posted the best times in the world for the 100-meter butterfly. It was a fabulous race. Spectators were engaged. The television announcers called the event with unguarded enthusiasm. Somehow, Phelps managed a last second surge and touched the wall 1/100th of a second ahead of his competitors, in route to another gold medal.

Everyone knew nineteen-year-old Phelps entered the Athens games intent on chasing Mark Spitz's record of seven medals. The quest was still within reach. But then, Phelps shocked everyone by producing one of the most unexpected and memorable moments of the 2004 Olympics.

Immediately following the butterfly competition, Phelps and teammate Crocker sat together for a television interview. They both talked about the importance of team and how happy they were for each other. It was an unusual display of team spirit especially in light of some egotistical showboating and boasting on the part of other American athletes. Phelps and Crocker genuinely shared the spotlight and unpretentiously shared the glory of the moment. It was heartwarming and probably unprecedented.

Shortly thereafter, a special announcement shocked the Olympic world. Michael Phelps decided to step aside, allowing Crocker to swim in his place in the upcoming 400-meter relay. Phelps told the media Crocker was better in this event than he was and the team had a better chance to win with Crocker than with him. You're kidding! Even though he had earned the right to swim this event, he decided to give Crocker an opportunity to earn his own gold medal. When the buzzer sounded and the relay began, Phelps was in the stands, enthusiastically cheering on Crocker as the U.S. team went on to capture the gold.

Phelps's decision rocked the Olympic world. His concession made headlines around the world. Why? Because this display of selfless team spirit, is so rare in the athletic world. Or is it just the athletic world? Could it be rare in your world as well?

Team spirit is all about understanding that we succeed

only to the degree we help our team succeed. G.K. Chesterton is credited with saying, "There is the great man who makes every man feel small, but the really great man is the man who makes every man feel great."

Team spirit—the realization by each team member that they are only as good as their team's ability to succeed. That's powerful stuff!

Howard Hendricks said, "You can impress people from a distance, but you can only impact them close up."

> When it comes to your teammates, you want to compete in such a way that instead of *competing* with them, you are *completing* them. Those are two different mind-sets.
> —JOHN MAXWELL

One way that we can inspire a team spirit is to get close to the people that we work with. What can you do to get more comfortable with your co-workers? Take time to get to know people. Discover what's important to them. Seek to understand their ideas, feelings, opinions, beliefs and values. Get inside of their world. Let others know how much you value them and appreciate all they do to help the team succeed.

In addition, let people see who you are. Be genuine. Be vulnerable. Be real. Listen to people's hearts. Share yours. Take time to connect with people. The more transparent you are the less people have to guess who you are or how you'll respond to situations. Express what's in your heart.

Be willing to give of yourself without expecting anything

in return. Whatever you want most for your team, be willing to give it. Speak positively about each other, your efforts and your achievements. Help each other win and take pride in each other's accomplishments. Go to great lengths to help each other be right – not wrong.

The news headlines read: "The Miracle at Quecreek." Nine miners, trapped for three days 240 feet underground in a water-filled mine shaft, "decided early on they were either going to live or die as a group."

The fifty-five-degree water was the perfect formula for death by hypothermia. One news report recounted the miner's experience: "When one would get cold, the other eight would huddle around the person and warm that person, and when another person got cold, the favor was returned."

Everybody had strong moments," miner Harry B. Mayhugh told reporters after being released from Somerset Hospital in Somerset, Pennsylvania. "But

> The difference between an average player and a great player is your willingness to sacrifice for your teammates.
>
> —CHARLES GARFIELD

any certain time maybe one guy got down, and then the rest pulled together. And then that guy would get back up, and maybe someone else would feel a little weaker, but it was a team effort. That's the only way it could have been."*

* From Brian Palmer, Jeff Flock, and Jeff Goodell, "Quecreek Miner Miracle: Teamwork Helped Miners Survive Underground," 28 July 2002. Found at www.CNN.com /2002/US/07?28 mine-accident.

Miracle of miracles...they all came out alive - together.

Huddle together, support, trust, sacrifice unselfishly, and you will build a world class team that lands on top—together.

CHAPTER 9

IT'S TIME TO FLY

C. WILLIAM FISHER, in his book, *Don't Park Here*, tells about driving in his car with his 4-year-old son. "Byron, what do you want to be when you grow up to be a man?" he inquired. The youngster replied, "I don't want to grow up to be a man." Surprised, his father asked, "Why not?" Byron replied, "Because then I couldn't ride my tricycle!"

Fisher wrote, "As I drove on, I thought, 'I'm sure I enjoyed my tricycle when I was 4, but I'm also sure that I enjoy much more the power and performance of my Olds (probably a Toyota in current times) today.'"

Fisher's point reminds me of the two caterpillars crawling across the grass when a beautiful butterfly flew over. One nudged the other and commented, "You couldn't get me up in one of those things for a million dollars!"

Neither the caterpillar nor little Byron understood the excitement of growth. How many times do we cling to childhood tricycles or limited performance, not realizing the potential for so much more? To get what you want out of life, you will be required to continually change and grow. Personal growth transforms life through the development of powers not yet recognized.

Growth is preceded by substantial effort. There is no shortcut. An unceasing effort to advance, move forward, and explore the unknown will protect you from the trap of the tried and true. Growth doesn't come conveniently packaged in a microwave container that can be zapped and ready to serve. If you want to become all you can be, understand that explosive growth requires a commitment to a lifestyle of pursuing uncharted territories.

Here are a few stimulators to activate the growth process and overcome that fleeting thought of coasting.

Becoming all you can be is a mindset, a way of thinking. You must believe there is room for improvement and growth. When you rethink how you think, your mental boundaries will be stretched, expanding the room for your performance potential and eliminating perceived constraints.

The capacity to grow begins in your mind. Give yourself permission to risk the unknown.

> You've got to continue to grow or you're just like last night's corn bread -- stale and dry.
> —LORETTA LYNN

Growth requires you to abandon the status quo and overused methodologies. Sticking to the tried and true will stymie your ability to move beyond where you are. It is a subtle trap that keeps you living in a box. Instead, determine to abandon the usual and ignore doing what you've always done. Disturb your comfortable lifestyle. Do something new!

Be prepared for the long haul. There is no overnight success. Pursuing your potential will take considerable quiet, unapplauded effort. It is an inside job that defies discouragement and survives without public recognition. An old Irish proverb says, "You've got to do your own growing, no matter how tall your grandfather is." In other words, you can't depend on what others before you have done or your past performance to guarantee future brightness.

Surround yourself with people who are vitally alive and stretching. Stay away from boring people who live in a grave with ends knocked out—a rut. Get close to those who epitomize a passion for the privilege of living and the pursuit of possibilities.

Dissolve the perfectionist mandate. The pursuit of perfectionism can be mobilizing. The demand for perfection can be immobilizing and paralyzes progress. The demand for perfection cripples your ability to move ahead because nothing will ever be "good enough" to build on. Perfectionism often becomes an excuse not to try at all. Growth is not a finished product but a way of making each part of our life better. Perfectionists are continually looking to achieve unblemished results. It's not going to happen.

Continually dream, plan, create new goals and identify new challenges to conquer. Stagnant living is being over concerned with obstacles and limitations. Replace old expectations with new aspirations by pursuing the unknown. You will be motivated to expand yourself to meet new challenges and master new approaches. Ronald E. Osborne stated, "Unless you do something beyond what you've already mastered, you will never grow."

Stop doing something you presently do. More of the same just produces more of the same. Evaluate your beliefs, habits, and behaviors. Determine what isn't working or adding substantial value to your life. Eliminate it. Replace it. No matter how hard you try to make the old methods work, you will reach a point of diminishing returns. An addiction to the old makes it virtually impossible to learn anything new.

Be willing to make mistakes. Growth requires you to learn on the go, right through your mistakes and failures. Errors are expected, even welcomed. Take advantage of them. They are ever present learning tools, warning signals and detour signs that keep us on course to personal success.

Eliminate excuses. "I'm too old to start now." "I'm set in my ways." "I'm just too comfortable where I am even though I'm not getting the results I want." I've heard them all and a hundred others. Every excuse is a good excuse but not one is acceptable. Take charge. Make choices. Eliminate excuses. You are in control.

George Eliot wrote, "It is never too late to be what you might have become." There is no time like the present to get started. Growth doesn't begin until you do. You must move...take action...mobilize your resources...eliminate resistors and channel your energies to push your personal effectiveness to an all-time high.

How the Best Keep Getting Better

In the late 1600s, three rural families dominated the musical instrument industry. Working in shops located side-by-side in the Italian village of Cremona, these families produced the finest in violins.

The Amatis family hung a sign outside their shop that read: "The best violins in all Italy." Not wanting their creations to go unnoticed, the Guarnerius family posted a sign that read: "The best violins in all the world!" The famous Anton Stradivari, known to produce the finest, most expensive stringed instrument, boasted his worldwide notoriety by hanging a sign on his front door which simply read: "The best violins on the block!"

Stradivari was a self-taught violin making perfectionist. He refused to develop a relationship with "good enough." Using primitive tools and working alone until late in life, Stradivari created a standard of violin quality unmatched by his competitors. Each violin had to meet his personal standards. His passionate attention to detail allowed him to make the bold statement; "Other people will make other violins, but no one shall make a better one."

Can you make that same claim? Other people may do what you do, but no one will do it better. Henry Ward Beecher suggested, "Hold yourself responsible for a higher standard than anybody else expects of you. Never excuse yourself." To be the best you can be requires an unquenchable desire to continually make your best better. The exciting result is that your commitment to personal excellence will last a lifetime and beyond.

"Once you're labeled 'the best,'" said Larry Bird during his prime in the NBA, "you want to stay up there, and you can't do it by loafing around." In his off-season, Larry Bird lifted weights, ran, and worked on new moves and shots. "If I don't keep changing," Bird told Esquire magazine, "I'm history."

Are you the best? What effort are you putting forth to get there, and, if there, how are you refining your skills to make sure you don't become unfortunate "history"?

The best keep getting better.

> The quality of an individual is reflected in the standards they set for themselves.
> —RAY KROC

Jessica Tandy, Oscar winner for her role in *Driving Miss Daisy*, was asked in Vis a Vis if any of her performances have left her unsatisfied. "All of them," she instantly replied. "I've never come off the stage at the end of a performance and said, 'Tonight, everything was perfect.' There'll always be some little thing that I'll have to get right tomorrow." Such is the reason why her performance in the movie *Fried Green Tomatoes* once again won her outstanding reviews.

Are you raising the bar on your current idea of excellence? The best keep redefining better.

No one knows for sure who invented the cupcake, but

there's no question who improved it. D.R. "Doc" Rice is credited with injecting the cream filling and putting the squiggly white line atop the cupcake's chocolate icing at Continental Baking Company's Detroit Plant. Rice's changes in the original devil's food cake hand-covered with vanilla or chocolate icing formula, led to widespread popularity of the snack.

What areas of your life could become better with an 'injection' of innovative thought and action?

The best make things better and raise the bar.

Michelangelo received a visit from a friend as he worked diligently on a sculpture. After a brief chat, the friend left but returned later to find Michelangelo working on the same statue. Thinking the statue was nearly completed on his last visit and seeing no visible change, he exclaimed, "You haven't been working all this time on that same statue, have you?"

"Indeed I have," the sculptor replied. "I've been retouching the facial features, refining the leg muscles, polishing the torso; I've softened the presentation of some areas and enhanced the eye's expression."

"But all those things are insignificant," responded the visitor. "They are mere trifles." "That may be," replied Michelangelo, "but trifles make perfection, and perfection is no trifle."

"Trifles make perfection and perfection is no trifle." I love that concept! Although simply spoken, the consequences have monumental impact. People who pay attention to the "little things," the seemingly insignificant, produce excellence in larger matters. The best pay attention to the trifling details.

Take inventory. What small details in your life have you overlooked? Are there functions that appear insignificant? Renew your commitment and give attention to these finishing touches.

The self-esteem, growth, satisfaction, and fulfillment you experience at work depend on you. To transform your daily "have-to's" into a lifestyle of "want-to's," consider these two questions: *"What do I want out of my life's work?"* and *"What am I willing to do to make it happen?"*

If you love what you do and love the people you work with, you'll never have to work another day in your life.

IF YOU'RE A FAN OF THIS BOOK, PLEASE TELL OTHERS...

- Write about *Playbook* on your blog. Post excerpts to your social media sites such as: Facebook, Twitter, Pinterest, Instagram, etc.
- Suggest *Playbook* to friends
- When you're in a bookstore, ask them if they carry the book. The book is available through all major distributors, so any bookstore that does not have it in stock can easily order it.

- Write a positive review on www.amazon.com.
- Purchase additional copies to give away as gifts

You can order additional copies of the book from your local bookstore or from my website by going to www.enthusedaboutlife.com. Special bulk quantity discounts are available.

Check out my other books to help maximize your effectiveness and impact at home, at work in the relationships that matter most...

Tinker

Discover the secrets for achieving excellence in our fast-paced, ever changing, chaotic world.

Celebrate

Harness the power of a new attitude and discover a life beyond your wildest dreams.

To order these books, go to my website: www.enthusedaboutlife.com

Additional Resources...

My first three book series can give you 12 simple secrets to a variety of life's goals. To find out more, and order copies, go to www.enthused about life.com

The Speaker's Sourcebook II duo will help you gain confidence in front of a crowd. To find out more, visit www.enthusedaboutlife.com.

Love Is A Verb is about those simple, yet often forgotten, accumulations of little actions that contribute to building our relationships into what we want them to become. To find out more, visit www.enthusedaboutlife.com or www.simpletruths.com.